Daisy Buchanan—beautiful, wealthy Long Island socialite. She is married to Tom and is the object of Gatsby's desire.

...............He is obsessed with Daisy, with whom he was in love before the war.

DAISY BUCHANAN

JAY GATSBY

Plate 1

Tom Buchanan— Daisy's philandering husband. He is wealthy, arrogant, and physically powerful and likes to play polo.

Myrtle Wilson— Tom's girlfriend. She is desperate to escape an unhappy marriage that lacks the wealth and status she wants, which leads to tragic consequences.

TOM BUCHANAN

MYRTLE WILSON

Plate 2

Nick Carraway— the book's narrator. He is Daisy's cousin and Gatsby's less well-off neighbor and best friend.

Jordan Baker— Daisy's friend. She is a professional golfer and is dating Nick.

NICK CARRAWAY

JORDAN BAKER

Plate 3

DAISY

Plate 4

DAISY

Plate 5

DAISY

Plate 6

DAISY

Plate 7

DAISY

Plate 8

GATSBY

Plate 9

GATSBY

Plate 10

TOM

Plate 11

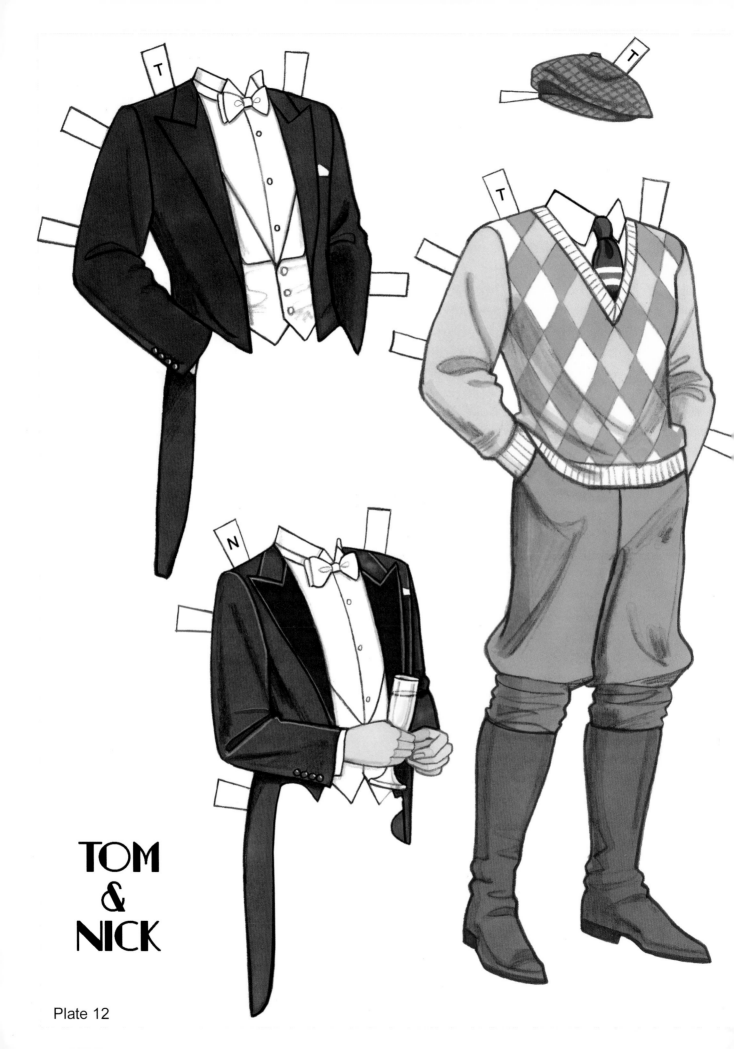

TOM
&
NICK

Plate 12

MYRTLE

Plate 13

JORDAN

Plate 14

JORDAN

Plate 15

NICK

Plate 16